NICOLAS DE STAËL

by Guy Dumur

CROWN PUBLISHERS, INC. - NEW YORK

Title Page: NICOLAS DE STAËL
Photography

Translated by:
FINTAN O'CONNELL

Series published under the direction of:
MADELEINE LEDIVELEC-GLOECKNER

Photography by:
HENRY B. BEVILLE, Annapolis Md. – JOHN EVANS, Ottawa – M. LACOSTE, Paris – OTTO NELSON, New York – M. ROUTHIER, Paris – ERIC SUTHERLAND, Minneapolis Minn. – JOHN TENNANT, Washington D.C. – JOHN WEBB, London

Black and White Illustrations:
Plates by JACQUES DUBOURG

We wish to thank the owners of works by Nicolas de Staël which are reproduced in this book.

Museums:

National Gallery of Canada, Ottawa – Musée national d'Art moderne, Paris – Kunstsammlung Nordrhein-Westfalen, Düsseldorf – Tate Gallery, London – Kunsthaus, Zurich – Museum of Winterthur – Cincinnati Art Museum, Ohio – Hirshhorn Museum and Sculpture Garden, Smithsonian Institution, Washington, D.C. – Milwaukee Art Center, Wisc. – Museum of Fine Arts, Boston, Mass. – Phillips Collection, Washington, D.C. – Walker Art Center, Minneapolis, Minn.

Galleries:
Stephen Hahn Gallery, New York

Private collections:

Prince Igor Troubetzkoy, Paris – Douglas Cooper, England – Dr. Nigel Weiss, London – Mr. and Mrs. Oscar Weiss, London – Mrs. Beatrice Glass, New York – Mr. and Mrs. John Lefebre, New York – Marion Lefebre Burge, New York – The late Hans Popper, San Francisco, Calif. – Mr. and Mrs. Jack I. Poses, New York – David N. Solinger, New York

Library of Congress Cataloging in Publication Data
Staël, Nicolas de, 1914–1955.
    Nicolas de Staël.

    1. Staël, Nicolas de, 1914–1955.   2. Painters–
France–Biography.   I. Dumur, Guy, 1921–   II. Ti-
tle.
ND553.S8D8413   759.4 [B]   76–27652
ISBN 0-517-52611-5

PRINTED IN ITALY – © 1975 BY BONFINI PRESS CORPORATION, NAEFELS, SWITZERLAND – ENGLISH TRASLATION © 1976
ALL RIGHTS OF REPRODUCTION OF ILLUSTRATIONS BY A.D.A.G.P., PARIS
ALL RIGHTS IN THE U.S.A. RESERVED BY CROWN PUBLISHERS, INC., NEW YORK, N.Y.

Composition « Astronomy », 1944   Oil, 40½″ × 94½″
Collection of Prince Igor Troubetzkoy, Paris

« A summit; an elemental; a shining candelabrum; a foundation; a majestic vertical; a fulsomeness; a prehension; this weaving texture like a shoal reef; an eternal, interior thunder; a chaos of things that precedes creation; a disciplined disorderliness; a palpable substance; a grumble; pictures armed with disarmingness; a story told in direct speech when one would have sworn it could only be related indirectly; an uneasiness; worn but intact; exempt from dimensions; a perpetual orphan. Here we have some possible and impossible equivalents of this alarming painting. »

For those who knew him these excerpts from a descriptive litany by Pierre Lecuire[1] form an exact portrait of Nicolas de Staël. « Elemental, » « shining candelabrum, » « disciplined disorderliness, » « uneasiness, » « worn but intact, » « perpetual orphan » correspond so exactly to what Nicolas de Staël was around 1950 that we may doubt that these expressions apply, as Lecuire would have it, only to the man's painting. If such were the case, then it means that Nicolas de Staël is visible in all his work. And not only because one recognizes his style at every moment in his short career, but because he painted with his entire being. Nicolas de Staël was an ontological painter.

He is the artist of our time who has come closest to the *essence* of painting, to such a point that his life and death became intermingled with it. Certainly, one can think of other painters from the past who struggled with this angel and lost their lives. But when Staël made his appearance around 1944–1945, he was the only one — and remains the only one — who

[1] *Voir Nicolas de Staël* (1953).

5

Composition, 1942   Pastel, 8½" × 12"   Private collection

could not be satisfied by skepticism and its intellectual or decorative corollaries which characterized the most successful works of his period, especially in France and the U.S.A. Conscious as he doubtless was like everyone else, of being at the end of a development, which for him began with the Russian icons and the mosaics at Ravenna and was completed by Braque and Matisse, he did all that he could to ensure that this supreme explosion, this tragedy, would owe nothing to historical chance nor even to his own life.

His friend René Char said that if one had to destroy one had to do it « with nuptial implements. » Nicolas de Staël destroyed nothing nor did he abolish anything which he did not re-create with the same instinctive movement — « the disciplined disorderliness » which Lecuire mentioned — as if the completion of a painting should never mean the destruction of everything it had stood for. His work is a convulsion, a cry, but one where death is indistinguishable from birth. Unlike Van Gogh, to whom he has often been compared, Nicolas de Staël did not make his

6

paintings his biography. It was not just the resources of Abstractionism that helped him to avoid the anecdotal, no matter how noble or pathetic they were, but it was also the quality of his commitment, which a violent — and up to now an incomprehensible — death then made absolute. His suicide is also that of painting. But neither of these joint deaths was the result of failure. They cast no slur on the success of a work, and a life that one must believe could only have been accomplished within a brief, explosive and compressed period of time. And this is where Nicolas de Staël's destiny becomes a part of history. The equation has only one unknown factor which in other days would have been called « genius.» The being and the doing, the painter and his painting are inseparable and, at the same time, antagonists.

This hand-to-hand struggle lasted barely ten years. Symbolically, it was the night Jacob spent struggling with the Angel. A fraction of life which becomes immense when one knows what went before and what came later to terminate it. It had of necessity, to be brief. The immeasurable is outside time. When Nicolas de Staël found out what he had to be, only ten years remained to him. In retrospect, it is this haste which one should seek to recognize in his paintings, like the accumulation of some energy which cannot spend itself for long without losing something of its substance or, again, of its being. The only gift which Nicolas de Staël lacked, and which could have helped him last longer, was guile.

Youth and Exile

Strength he had, and to spare. He was a big man — huge — with a deep, bass voice that was incredibly Russian. His face was long, very handsome and at the same time both sad and gay. His expressions seemed to retain something of childhood or a longing for the past. Impatient more than anguished, he was given to sudden rages and bouts of touchy pride and was quick to take offense, often for the most obscure reasons.

He could offer and withdraw his friendship with equal ease while still being capable of great constancy. Above all, he was unbelievably generous. He was devoid in my opinion, of any sense of possessiveness even as regards his own paintings, which is rather unusual in painters. A bad sleeper who often painted by electric light, he was also given to overindulgence in stimulants to keep him awake. Exaggerated in his speech as well as his acts, he was curious about everything. But interest soon turned to scorn, especially as regarded other painters. It was as if he could not bear the idea that others could be painters at the same time as himself. He was an ascetic, at least as far as those things which most people covet are concerned and, even after he had grown « rich,» he frequently dressed in clothes picked up in bargain sales at the Carreau du Temple. He was the very opposite of a middle-class gentleman.

He was basically proud of his heritage which blended the aristocracies of both breeding and talent. Frequently absent when he was actually present, he seems to have been in a perpetual flight of movement; walking, swimming, traveling. Inconstant, elusive and contradictory, he was a man built on a large scale who was not at ease in his own epoch. It was as if he had come from another world.

As the genealogists put it, his family tree was one of the oldest in Europe. When one questioned him about it he would haughtily reply: «Look it up in the Swedish Gotha.» The Staël-

Portrait of Jeannine, 1939   Charcoal, 11¼″ × 11″   Private collection, Paris

PORTRAIT OF JEANNINE, 1942   Oil, 33½″ × 25⅝″   Private collection, Paris ▷

8

LIGHT FRAGMENTS
1946
Oil, 39½″ × 25½″
Private collection
Paris
◁

▷
COMPOSITION
1946
Oil, 45½″ × 35″
Private collection
Paris

10

COMPOSITION IN BLACK, 1946   Oil, 78½″ × 59″   Kunsthaus, Zurich

Composition, 1943   Charcoal, 13" × 8½"   Private collection, Paris

COMPOSITION
1947
Oil, 45½″ × 28½″
Private collection
Zurich
◁

▷
MARATHON
1948
Oil, 32″ × 25½″
Tate Gallery
London

14

Holsteins are mentioned as being in Westphalia in the eighth century but toward the end of the twelfth century they were settled on the shores of the Baltic. As a result of the accidents of history, some of them became Swedish (and one recalls that the husband of Germaine Necker brought the name « de Staël » into French literature) while the others became Russian. Nicolas belonged to the latter branch. His father was an army officer and governor of the famous Fortress of SS. Peter and Paul in St. Petersburg where Nicolas was born in 1914, the fruit of his father's second marriage late in life. At the age of two Nicolas de Staël was already a page at the Court of Emperor Nicolas II. One year later the Russian Revolution broke up this world and General Vladimir de Staël, his wife and three children, Marina, Nicolas and Olga, were forced to flee from Russia to Poland. The father died in 1921 at the age of sixty-eight and the mother died near Danzig the following year. At that time Nicolas was seven and his sisters nine and five respectively.

They were put in the care of a Russian family in Brussels, called Fricero, who were rich, hospitable and more than sensitive to the miseries afflicting these poor exiles, victims of a revolution which they themselves detested. Later, in Paris, Nicolas de Staël would have as his tutor Léon Daudet whom he reproached for understanding nothing about painting. The Friceros were his real parents. In letters written during his adolescent years when he had already embarked on his vagabond life, he addressed them as *Papa* and *Maman*. With this family he and his sisters received the same sort of education they would have got at the Royal Court: training in aristocratic sports, private schools and serious studies. The latter however, did not prevent Nicolas de Staël, who was a great letter writer, from having difficulties with spelling all his life. His culture was visual and his reading was haphazard. He was more likely to be struck by a particular detail, image or a phrase than by a book as a whole. But he was drawn to certain writers, especially those who were interested in painting, such as Maurice Saillet, Georges Limbour, Georges Duthuit, Jean Grenier, Pierre Lecuire and René Char. The fact is, Nicolas de Staël was never an intellectual if this is understood as being someone who bases his life on reasoning, ideas and the written word. His birth and education (which he always affected to reject or to wish to abolish) belie the notion that he was any kind of autodidact. But he was too much the painter not to be suspicious of the universe of words even though he could easily have been a poet.

Like Delacroix, he was very fond of music and, in the last years of his life would think nothing of driving through the night from the south of France just to attend a concert in Paris. He would have liked to have worked with musicians and hoped (in vain) that Stravinsky and then Messiaen would compose a ballet based on a story by Char. He was one of the most assiduous spectators at the first nights of Pierre Boulez and the « Domaine Musical. »

This taste for music would seem to indicate that Nicolas de Staël chose to live in a world of sensations from the roughest to the most elaborate. He seems to have hungered for all that life could immediately offer him, and what could be more powerful than the images offered by painting?

Nevertheless, the source of Nicolas de Staël's vocation remains mysterious — but is it any more so than that of other painters? It all depends. When at the age of ten, Staël entered the Jesuit College of Saint-Michel in Brussels, he got more or less the same education which would have prepared him to become a cadet at St. Petersburg. It was not just pure chance that at this time he was an expert fencer. His adoptive father, Emmanuel Fricero, was the son of a naval attaché and engineer and he hoped that the young Nicolas would follow the same career. But by the time he was sixteen he was already passionately fond of painting, having seen at least one important exhibition of Belgian artists in Brussels and, a year later, the Rembrandts in the museums. He took up painting and soon sold a watercolor to a fisherman from Nieuport. During a trip to France in 1933 he got a bad reception from his uncle in the south of that country, Alexis Ivanovitch de Staël,

TRAPPED ROCKS, 1948
Oil, 15″ × 18⅛″   Cincinnati Art Museum, Cincinnati, Ohio

18   *Composition, 1946   Charcoal, 17″ × 10½″   Private collection*

ex-aide-de-camp to the Grand Duke Nicolas. Could this have been because the nephew was already taking lessons in drawing and painting? Knowing the adult Nicolas de Staël one can easily imagine what the adolescent must have been like: Warm, cheeky and already prodigiously generous. Nevertheless, he was apparently a good student and two years after entering the academy he was collaborating with his instructor on frescoes for the Agriculture and Glass Pavilions in Brussels in 1935.

In the same year he set off with a friend on a long trip through Spain, mostly on foot, which took him from Extremadura to the Balearic Islands.

We have some gouaches from this period which are marked by great precision in their execution: Boats in a harbor; «tachist» visions of churches that recall the paintings of Victor Hugo. Like Delacroix a hundred years before him, his letters bear witness to his enthusiasms:

«... Toledo is magnificent. We were camping on the banks of the Tagus and for more than eight days we soaked up the atmosphere. You end up telling the time from the shadows in the street like an old Toledo resident and El Greco holds no more secrets for us who have seen him every day....» At Guadalupe he doesn't mention the Zurbarán but he embraces the whole town: «Ramparts, turrets, courtyards, churches, undescribable, it all penetrates your innermost being and I don't know how to put it, but it never leaves you.... Divine moments. A swirl of emotions. I wish I were Barrès to explain it all to you.»[1]

When describing Andalusia and the dancing (which he compares to the images on Greek vases) it is less in the accents of Barrès that he expresses himself than in the style of those painter travelers of the nineteenth century. Everything is romantic in these letters and in the journey itself, including the visit he made to Villefranche-de-Rouergue to see his sister Olga who had become a nun in the convent of the Holy Family. Painting for one, the cloister for the other; it must have been a thirst for the absolute in these two émigré orphans that made them refuse a «normal» integration into a society which no matter what they may have tried to do, would always have been foreign to them. The upheavals that marked their childhood would seem to correspond, especially for Nicolas, to the fall of the Napoleonic Empire which in Western Europe, preceded and engendered the Romantic era.

In 1936 Nicolas de Staël set off on his travels again and this time he went to Morocco. Paris, which had now become the only city in the world where international painting flourished, had not yet attracted him. He had seen the Louvre, and Cézanne. But for the moment he preferred to follow in the footsteps of Delacroix, whose style is reflected in his correspondence where descriptions of the picturesque are mingled with concerns connected with painting:

«... One has to find some explanation why it is that one finds beautiful that which is beautiful. A technical explanation. It is indispensable, to know the rules of color, to know exactly why Van Gogh's apples at The Hague which are of a definitely crapulous local color seem so splendid, why Delacroix slashed his decorative ceiling nudes with rays of green and yet these same nudes are clear and have brilliant color to their flesh, why Veronese, Velasquez, Franz Hals all had more than 27 blacks and as many whites, Van Gogh committed suicide, Delacroix died hating himself, and Hals drank in despair, why, what was it? Their drawings? For a small canvas of Van Gogh in The Hague Museum we have two pages of his notes on its orchestration. Each color has its reason for

---

[1] This letter, as well as all the others quoted, is taken from a remarkable descriptive catalog, published in 1968 by « Le Temps » publishing house and which lists de Staël's paintings as established by Jacques Dubourg and Françoise de Staël. The introduction is by André Chastel. These letters are annotated with great precision by Germain Viatte.

RUE GAUGUET, ·1949
Oil on wood, 78½″ × 94¾″   Museum of Fine Arts, Boston, Mass.

20

COMPOSITION IN GREY AND BLUE, 1950
Oil, 45¼″ × 76¾″   Private collection, Paris

Composition, 1946   Wash, India ink, 24¾″ × 18½″   Private collection

existing and I, by God, I'd go to scan canvases without having studied and this because everyone is in a hurry, God knows why. . . . »

One notes the references. Would Nicolas de Staël have remained a belated follower of the painters he mentions or do these names (to whom the younger generation no longer dare even refer any more) simply imply an impossible yearning for the past? It is certainly true that if de Staël had only drawn and painted these views of Spain and Morocco and the « Icons » he showed in Brussels in 1936, we would probably recognize him only as a sensitive young man who would like at all cost, to escape from his own epoch. Even so, it is difficult not to notice this approach as well as phrases such as the following: « The sweet life for me is in working, in being uneasy, in reading, and my work doesn't much resemble the sweetness of the country. . . . »

Morocco at that time was full of second-rate painters who found life comfortable in the lodgings provided by Lyautey in excellent dwellings. Nicolas de Staël could have been but one among the many. Scarcely anything of interest survives from this gestation period. Yet everything will be found again later in a body of work which, from the solitude experienced in the midst of one of the most beautiful countries in the world, preserves a spiritual quality and a color sense which could have been acquired only through a direct contact with reality.

Nicolas de Staël's solitude in Morocco was interrupted when he fell in love with a young woman painter, Jeannine Guillou, who was already the mother of a little boy who later became the poet Antoine Tudal.

Staël had gone to Morocco, and supported himself there with money provided by a Belgian patron on the strength of the paintings he was to send back. But when he then set out for Italy with Jeannine Guillou and her son he was without funds. And if Morocco was the place where he had meditated longest on painting, met the woman he loved and who was his inspiration, it was in Brittany (where he spent the summer of 1939) where thanks to her, he met Jean Deyrolle, Jeannine's cousin. In Paris he had spent three weeks in the studio of Fernand Léger without learning anything. So it was with Jeannine and Deyrolle that, at the age of twenty-five, he was to discover the possibilities of a new type of painting which he would exploit much later.

When war broke out the ex-page at the court of the Czar found himself in the Foreign Legion. He ended up at Sidi-bel-Abbès, Algeria, and then in Tunisia where with others like himself, he was employed in drawing maps for the staff. But this adventure did not last long since he was demobilized on September 19, 1940, and rejoined Jeannine in Nice. He was doing almost no painting at this period except (perhaps harking back to his adolescent dreams and memories of El Greco and Cézanne) for a few still lifes and, sometime in 1941–42 the admirable *Portrait of Jeannine* which makes one think simultaneously of El Greco and Picasso of the blue period.

At Nice he met Magnelli, Jean Klein, Marie Raymond, Le Corbusier, and it was here that his daughter Anne was born in 1942. This was a crucial year since it marked a turning point in his work which had not yet settled on the direction it was to take. In fact, if we except one or two still lifes and the *Portrait of Jeannine,* one can say that it was really only in 1942 that Nicolas de Staël began to paint. Nothing in his new works recalls the drawing, gouaches or sketches done before. Up until around 1950, most of Nicolas de Staël's canvases bore the title *Composition*. They owe nothing to reality, not even that reality which Picasso, Braque and Matisse had distorted.

In spite of the Cubist experience, the abstract trend in painting had not really caught on in France. The public, the dealers and the museums ignored Mondrian, Kandinsky (actually living in Paris), the Russian Supremists. Even Paul Klee who could have indicated a direction, was unknown. Paris had been the European capital of painting since the time of the Impressionists and had progressively assimilated the foreigners and brutally eliminated whatever else was not

«Nocturne,» 1950
Oil, 38″ × 57½″   Phillips Gallery, Washington, D.C.

«Le Lavandou,» 1952
Oil, 76¾″ × 38¼″
Musée national d'Art moderne, Paris

COMPOSITION, 1951
Oil, 28¾″ × 36″   Private collection, Zurich

COMPOSITION, 1951
Oil, 35″ × 45½″   Collection of David N. Solinger, New York

27

COMPOSITION ON RED GROUND, 1951
Oil, 21″ × 31¾″   Private collection, Paris

taking place on the spot. Outside of a small group of enthusiasts, the French in general were not much interested in painting. The rich middle classes bought the works of Utrillo, Vlaminck, Derain (of the later period) and Kisling. Picasso and Dali were known more for their peculiar personalities. Braque and Matisse lived solitary lives in isolation and Soutine died in poverty.

With the German Occupation things became better and, at the same time, worse. All the so-called « Modern » painters had been condemned by the Nazi regime and some of them, who had already been forced to flee from Germany, now ended up in the U.S.A. Those who remained behind could not show their works. The collaborationist press foretold the doom of decadent painting. But at the same time, and perhaps thanks to these attacks, growing numbers of art enthusiasts began to take an interest in the painting of their own time which, from Modigliani to Picasso, already had its legends. The studios of André Lhote and Fernand Léger were filled with a crowd of young painters now anxious to learn the old lessons of Cubism which had been rejected by the Cubists themselves. Most of the leading art dealers had been Jews and had had to flee, but others took their place. Jeanne Bucher was one of these and she became the first to take an interest in Nicolas de Staël.

A « Paris School » was in the course of developing, the first representatives of which were the semifigurative colorists: Estève, Bazaine, Lapicque, Pignon and Tal Coat, all of whom would be on the inside track during the years following the Liberation. So at the time Nicolas de Staël really began to paint — that is, 1942 — many painters of his generation had already seen that the evolution of painting was bound to pass through Abstractionism.

The Violence of Abstraction

Can one really speak of foreign inspiration, of the sudden discovery of a man such as Kandinsky? The frontiers were closed. Paradoxically, it was possibly the Occupation which not only encouraged a forbidden activity through sheer contrariness, but which also set the scene for a complete break with Surrealism and with the leaders of modern art: Braque, Matisse and Picasso, even though their followers were legion.

Nicolas de Staël did not discover Abstractionism on his own any more than anyone else did. But his meetings with Deyrolle and with Magnelli, Sonia Delaunay and Jean Arp at Nice enabled him to make the break. As we have already said he forgot what he had been and became someone else, although it cannot be said that he immediately turned into the great painter he was to become a few years later. The paintings of 1943 are free compositions where the colors are certainly emphasized, but they are still subject to a severity — not to say stiffness — of outline. One cannot speak of geometric abstraction, as in the case of Mondrian and his successors: Dewasne, Vasarely, Magnelli — but rather of a style which was both precise and uncertain; which hesitated between the freedom of the artist and the decorative concerns which were encouraged by the innate good taste that never deserted Nicolas de Staël.

The important point is that a style be defined and take on breadth. In 1944, the « compositions » which were shown in a group exhibition at Jeanne Bucher's (where Staël was symbolically hung between Magnelli and Kandinsky) and those shown at his first private exhibition

Landscape, 1947   Drawing, 28¾″ × 41½″   Private collection

at L'Esquisse Gallery bear witness to something more than the craftsmanship one would expect from a thirty-year-old painter who had already spent half of these years reflecting on his art. The muted, almost dead colors, the fused geometric lines that are still legible, the slightly monotonous severity in the organization of the shapes and their relationships, speak of an equilibrium between a personality which is looking to establish itself and the coldness of an art which must, by definition, be impersonal.

      During these two or three years, depending on whether one considers 1944 or 1945, Nicolas de Staël renounced the earlier Romanticism (to which he would later return by a different route) to set off in a new direction, which one would have thought unusual for someone of his origins and temperament were it not for the fact that he was escorted on the way by two other Russians: Kandinsky (who died in 1944) and Lanskoy who was perhaps closer to him.

30

But if one can find in Lanskoy something of that Russian «Rayonnisme» with its violent colors and aggressive spirit of decoration, the art of Nicolas de Staël is tempered by the French tradition (he had copied Chardin at the Louvre) to which Nicolas always proclaimed his fidelity. Doubtless Braque, whom Nicolas de Staël got to know at this period and who illustrated a book of poems by the young son of Jeannine Guillou, was aware of this. Braque, in fact, was not particularly well disposed to younger painters and his friendship with Staël was probably of some significance. Staël, who was never close to Kandinsky, who detested Picasso, who was a passionate admirer of Matisse without ever trying to be like him, had chosen from among his famous elders this most «French» of painters; the one who immediately after the Liberation, would eclipse the glory of Picasso by making paintings of supreme refinement that were the direct opposite in spirit to the native violence of Nicolas de Staël. This admiration and friendship demonstrate a wish, never denied, to paint

Composition, 1948   Drawing (sheet 14" × 21") under visible passe-partout plate 10¾" × 17½"
Private collection

Untitled, 1944
Drawing, 17″ × 10½″
Collection
of Mr. and Mrs.
John Lefebre
New York

LANDSCAPE, 1952
Oil, 21¼″ × 28¾″   Collection of Marion Lefebre Burge, New York

33

«Parc des Princes,» 1952
Oil, 76¾″ × 38⅛″
Private collection, Paris
◁

▷
Football Players, 1952
Oil on cardboard, 13⅝″
× 10⅝″
Private collection, Paris

Figures at the Seaside, 1952   Oil, 63¼″ ×50¼″   Kunstsammlung Nordrhein-Westfalen, Düsseldorf

only with the means at the disposal of the painter, that is, outside all literary influence and (especially if we think of Chardin or more precisely Braque) without any consideration for the dramatic elements inherent in the «subject.»

The feeling of serenity that emerges from the «compositions» painted between 1942 and 1945 is in harsh contrast to the existence Nicolas de Staël was enduring at this same period. His meeting with Jeannine Guillou had marked the end of a roving adolescence protected by his adopted parents. The year spent in the Foreign Legion, the move to Nice and then Paris (where he lived for the first time) entailed hard realities. With the responsibility of a wife, her son and their own little daughter, Staël knew a poverty that was further aggravated by the difficulties of the Occupation. At Nice he took on the most humble jobs such as furniture polisher for a cabinetmaker and, in Paris, worked as a scene shifter at the Châtelet and as apprentice to the painter Fontanarosa, without ever really earning a living. Jeanne Bucher found only a few purchasers for his paintings but the basis for some firm friendships was laid at this period such as that with the industrialist Jean Bauret. Nevertheless, the Staël family suffered from cold and hunger and these privations certainly played their part in the eventual death of Jeannine Guillou, a death which Staël announced to his in-laws in a letter that is overwhelming in its simplicity. «...At 2: 45 this morning, Jeannine died on February 27, 1946, as a result of complications following an operation by the Head of the Beaudeloque Hospital to remove a child she had resigned herself not to keep. I cannot write to you otherwise. I have been able to buy a plot of four meters at the northern entrance to the Montrouge cemetery with a grant in perpetuity. . . .»

This death made him an orphan for the second time. He was never to forget Jeannine Guillou and was to find her again in his daughter Anne for whom he bore an exclusive love.

Before this tragedy broke over his head, the extreme poverty in which de Staël found himself as well as his worry over Jeannine, whom he knew to be in poor health, were both bound to be reflected somehow in his work, which he still pursued without interruption. From 1945, the style that he had discovered at the same moment as so many other painters of his generation suddenly began to explode. The rectangles, triangles and linear treatments, similar to the lead drawings on glazed windows, no longer sufficed. In March of that same year, 1945, Staël wrote to a collector, Jean Adrian:

«... I admit playing badly the role of the unconscious especially at a time when reason serves to filter the day, when the next day it propels all the filth which we think it is its duty to stop. It is very difficult for me to seize on the truth: it is more complicated and more simple than we imagine, and God knows if all this experience gets through to a poor man, but I want to repeat to what point I believe that when all the elements are there, the choice determined, the attitude passive, the will to organize order and chaos, all the requirements, all the possibilities, poverty and the ideal, in the best pictures everything goes off in such a way that one has the impression of not even having a word to say. ... On the subject of instinct we must have different concepts; for me instinct is unconscious perfection and my paintings live by conscious imperfection.»

As a matter of fact, this admirable letter was followed a month later by another type of appeal: «Jean, they are cutting off the gas and the water tomorrow, everything is happening at the same time and I can do nothing. Give two thousand francs to Antek [his stepson] until Monday. Please forgive and thanks.»

On the one hand we have the lofty demands of a restless soul; on the other the most dramatic aspects of a squalid life. The Romantics, such as Van Gogh, made this the very basis of their art. Staël, whose poverty never reached the depths of his contemporary Wols, no longer had

Untitled, 1948   Drawing, 17¾″ × 11″   Private collection

available the landscapes, objects and faces through which, up to then, the painter could express his personal tragedy. Staël can only resort to movement, chance and the void. Furthermore, the role of subjectivity is large in his compositions with colors that are generally somber — blacks, beiges, verdigrises — which have their own severity and transpose, from one to the other, a sort of lyric continuity that cannot be confused however, with «tachism,» «dripping» or the pictorial «acts» of painters who came after him. For the moment, the geometric element — which is entirely relative — of the paintings done between 1942 and 1945, was shattered; but we are still a very long way from Tobey, Rothko, Mathieu and Pollock.

The large composition done in 1946 entitled *On Dancing,* with its dull blues and its splashes of red, brings Staël closer to Braque and La Fresnaye. The «conscious imperfection» he speaks of in the previously cited letter relates to a French tradition which would seem to confirm his visit in the spring of 1946 to the exhibition of tapestries in Angers which included *The Lady with the Unicorn* and *The Apocalypse.* With thick streaky lines — which sometimes suggest ladders and sometimes bars — and ominous blacks and yellows, Staël had moved imperceptibly toward the glorification of pure painting. The violence of movement shows no sign of attenuation. It remains however, subject to imperative colors: Brick red perceived through the brown, gray-blue verging on black. The old order of «values» is respected. Abstraction becomes depth. Over a period of more than three years, through numerous paintings mostly done by electric light, Staël proves to us that abstract painting can express a temperament, that each canvas can follow its own rules and, at the same time still belong to the uninterrupted development and history of painting.

Up until the years 1949–50, therefore, one is aware of a self-confident evolution that is encouraged and favored by his new marriage, his moving into a spacious studio in Rue Gauguet, his friendship with Lanskoy, the timid approaches of a dealer such as Louis Carré (but their contract didn't lead to anything) and, most encouraging of all, recognition by a critic such as Pierre Courthion who is overwhelmed: «The joy of painting: the cuisine of a wizard. Nicolas de Staël immediately gets down to the essentials; to what makes a painter. Ingredients are fondled, stirred and transformed. With the posing of the color, the greedy density of the smeared substance, one can guess at his appetite to dismember his prey, to shred it to pieces with his teeth: The bogus ferocity of a man who has the rare distinction of being highly civilized and, for want of a narrow utilitarian moral, shows himself extremely respectful of the spiritual hierarchies. . . .» Pierre Courthion also recalls that Staël refused to be considered as an abstract painter and that «he always needs to have before his eyes, either close or afar, the restless source of his inspiration which is the sentient universe.» [1]

Upon what are these statements of Pierre Courthion based? We should note that more and more frequently the general term «composition» is now replaced by titles which refer to reality: *The Nest, Marathon, The Difficult Path,* «*L'eau de vie,*» *Trapped Rocks, Blue Forest,* «*Jour de fête,*» etc. In fact, these paintings do not suggest any different inspiration from those which have no title. The comparison made at the time, with the early pictures of Utrillo are not enough for us to speak of a «sentient reality.» Whether he argued with the epithet or not, Nicolas de Staël was an abstract painter — and in our view he will always remain so — entirely free from the exterior world. For him the pictorial art was, and remained, something complex and mysterious and he was so aware of this that he could cite to Pierre Courthion the following from a letter by Keats: «. . . I have ever been too sensible of the labyrinthian path to eminence in Art (judging from Poetry) ever to think I understood the emphasis of Painting. The innumerable compositions and decompositions

---

[1] Extracts from the catalog at the Staël exposition in Montevideo, Uruguay, 1948.

which take place between the intellect and its thousand materials before it arrives at that trembling delicate and snail-horn perception of Beauty — I know not you many havens of intenseness — nor ever can know them — but for this I hope not you atchieve [*sic*] is lost upon me: for when a Schoolboy the abstract Idea I had of an heroic painting — was what I cannot describe I saw it. . . . »[1]

One feels that Nicolas de Staël would have liked to have written this letter himself. Even if elsewhere he evokes «what is essentially organic, vital,» the forces that move him are not only sensorial. Abstract or not, his paintings above all represent a battle with painting. A strictly personal relationship between the utilization of colors, the bare canvas and the completed canvas. The overloading of his materials, for which Staël became more and more avid, reveals an attitude which seems partly ingenuous toward «the organic» and «the vital.» Not for nothing are the spatulas used by painters in place of brushes called «knives.» Be it trowel or knife, the giant Nicolas de Staël seems to be constructing and hewing the sticky materials which either mix together or, when the various coats have dried for several days or weeks, superimpose themselves on one another like geological strata, to give every effect of transparency. That which other painters achieved by fluidity, Staël got by a deceptive thickness which reveals the blue or the green under the gray just as on a tree the bark lies beneath the moss, and under the bark there is the smooth wood of the tree trunk. The transparency becomes the very opposite of preciosity. That good taste which Staël always demonstrated never gives way to decorative prettiness. What emerges from this accumulation of muted color seems to be an instrinsic will of the work to exist by and for itself. With Staël living, his paintings were inseparable from his personality. But since his death — and this is particularly true of the paintings done in 1949–50 — his works only exist by themselves. When Staël refused the description of abstract painter he reminds us of Delacroix refusing the definition of a Romantic: «Me, sir? — Why, I am a pure Classicist,» but he was the only one to know the secret of what he painted.

OPEN DOORS

Another innovation during this period was the discovery of the large format. And here again one could be tempted to draw a comparison between the size of certain paintings — 8 feet by 6½ feet for «*La Rue Gauguet*» (1949) — and the size of the painter. He was bound to invent a universe that would correspond to his size. But where one can see the degree of strength and maturity he has achieved is when he moves from the smaller to the larger format without having to alter manner or style. Yet a «big» painting by de Staël is not just the enlargement of a small one any more than the converse is so. This independent life of the paintings makes it almost seem that each composition fills the place it was destined to. And this is so true that later on, when Staël would allow himself to make preparatory studies, or bring back from a trip or a vision a series

[1] Letter to B. R. Haydon, April 8, 1818.
The Letters of John Keats, 1814–1821. Edited by Hyder Edward Rollins. Vol. I. Harvard University Press, Cambridge, Massachusetts, 1958.

40

NICE, 1954   Oil, 29″ × 36½″
Hirshhorn Museum and Sculpture Garden, Smithsonian Institution,
Washington, D.C.

STUDY AT LA CIOTAT, 1952
Oil, 13¾″ × 18″   Tate Gallery, London

BOTTLES IN THE STUDIO, 1952
Oil, 51″ × 35″   Private collection ▷

42

SEASCAPE, 1952
Oil, 31¾″ × 45½″   Collection of Mrs. Beatrice Glass, New York

44

of colored notes on scraps of paper, these sketches would bear no relation, either in style or form, with what the final painting would turn out to be. But the temptation to do things on a grand scale, to achieve, between 1950 and 1952, a painting 13 feet in width by 6½ feet high, such as the one the English collector and art critic Denys Sutton would buy, seems to have responded to a need for a grandiose affirmation which henceforth allowed for a sureness in touch and the perfect use of color.

Although the «big» dealers were not yet interested in Staël and although the contract with Louis Carré, in particular, did not lead to anything, we have seen that the material situation for the artist after 1946, was no longer marked by the tragedies of the previous years. His marriage to Françoise Chapouton and the birth of his daughter Laurence (1947) and his son Jérôme (1948) had a settling effect on Nicolas de Staël. He took up with well-known artists and writers, Georges Braque in particular, whom he saw regularly, then there was Lanskoy mentioned previously, and a young Spanish painter called Alonso. Among the writers his circle included Maurice Saillet, Georges Limbour and Georges Duthuit (Matisse's son-in-law), who wrote an essay on him in 1950: «The rings of the North uncoil and the steel tongue of its monsters twist and thrust toward Byzantium, under the direction of Nicolas de Staël emerging with his broadsword from some out-sized icon....» Critics such as Pierre Courthion and Roger Van Gindertaël had already praised him to the skies in 1948, preceding the important critical bibliography that would develop from 1950 on. The Dominicans of Saulchoir included him in an exhibition along with Adam, Braque, Lanskoy and Laurens. Nicolas de Staël was now no longer alone.

In 1947 he had already met the American dealer Theodore Schempp who lived above the Staëls in the Rue Gauguet. Schempp was a true pioneer who made a breakthrough in the United States and Staël soon figured in one of the most prestigious collections in that country, the Phillips Gallery of Washington.

But it was mostly as a result of his meeting with Jacques Dubourg in 1949 that Nicolas de Staël very quickly became the favorite painter of the fifties.

Jacques Dubourg was one of those major dealers on Boulevard Haussmann who, up till then, had been interested only in proven values. Careful and prudent in both speech and judgment, Jacques Dubourg certainly did not possess the daring and imagination which in that era, characterized the prodigious discoverer of talent, René Drouin, in whose gallery at the Place Vendôme one could see Fautrier, Dubuffet, Wols, Max Ernst, «L'Art brut». All had the active blessings of Tapié de Celeyran and Jean Paulhan. The Dubourg-Staël relationship had very much the quality of that between a father and son. Although he was an art dealer who was clearly working in his own interests as well as those of de Staël, Jacques Dubourg was still considerably more than just that. He was completely charmed by de Staël and with him he lived the great adventure of his life, but with a discretion, modesty and generosity that remained unsullied then and after. This was most unusual, both for a dealer and for Nicolas de Staël who as we have said before, was quick to take offense, and no biography should let this fact go by unnoticed.

The «success» of Nicolas de Staël from 1950 onward can also be explained by historic reasons. This was the period when critics and patrons realized that they could no longer afford to ignore a pictorial phenomenon which the more timid souls — or interested parties — were still trying to oppose. The painters who were later to form «L'Ecole de Paris» and found the «Salon de mai» were almost in agreement. A few stale whiffs of Surrealism — but André Breton would now like to meet Nicolas de Staël — the wrath of some old dullards (not to mention the little heeded orders of «social realism») cannot overcome a movement long found to be irreversible. Abstractionism can cover different methods, sensibilities and sources of inspiration, from Monet of the *Waterlilies*

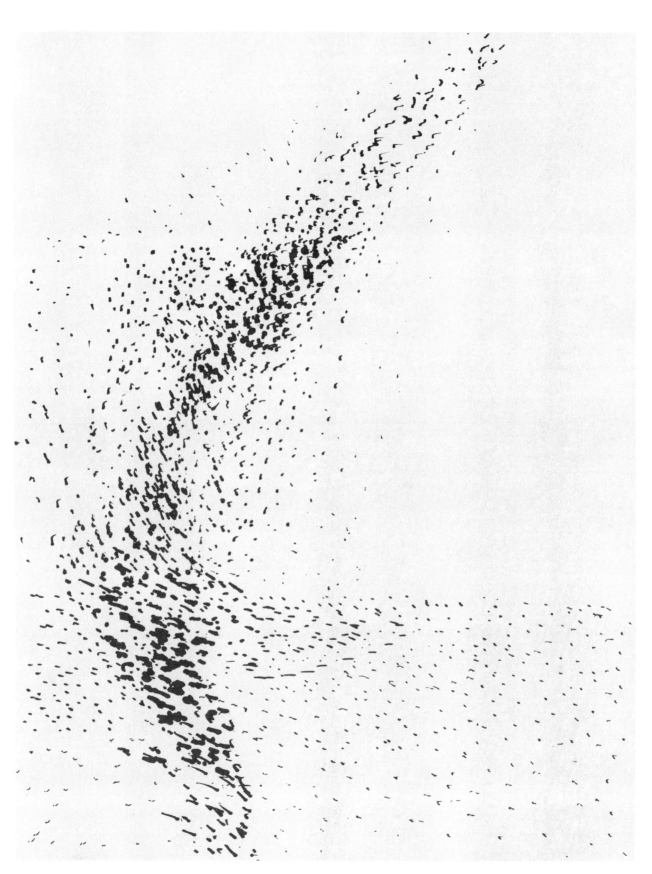

Birds in Flight, 1951 Felt-tipped pen on paper, 28″ × 20¾″ Phillips Gallery, Washington, D.C.

Pointillist Landscape, 1951   Drawing, 20⅞″ × 29⅛″   Private collection

to Kandinsky or Mondrian, and henceforth it is the unique resort of painting which in this, only slightly precedes the rise of Atonalism and Serialism in music.

  For Staël, the first big exhibitions began to follow one another in New York, Paris and London. He takes his place in the Paris Museum of Modern Art, and enters all the major English and American collections. Articles about him come next and books are already being written. He is welcomed everywhere without ever losing that air of a Cossack officer in exile — violent and refined, wildly generous. Unable to bear loneliness — except when working and this he does preferably by night. He is willing to walk across the whole of Paris to seek out a friend, and his curiosity is boundless. After a childhood spent in Belgium and long stays in Spain, Morocco, Italy and Nice; after the hard apprenticeship years in Paris, he now discovers London with amazement. This leads him to declare that he now has affinities only with northern countries and northern light.

Untitled, 1951   Drawing, 26¼″ × 20¾″   Private collection

THE PARK OF SCEAUX, 1952   Oil, 63¾″ × 44¾″   Phillips Gallery, Washington, D.C.

LANDSCAPE, LA CIOTAT, 1952
Oil, 31½″ × 31½″ Collection of David N. Solinger, New York

RED SKY, 1952
Oil, 51³/₁₆ × 63³/₄   Walker Art Center, Minneapolis, Minn.

FLOWERS ON BLACK GROUND, 1952   Oil, 51″ × 35″
Collection of the late Hans Popper, San Francisco, Calif.

LANDSCAPE, 1952   Oil, 13″ × 16″
Stephen Hahn Gallery, New York

53

STANDING NUDE
1953
Oil, 57″ × 35″
Private collection
Paris
◁

▷
«LES INDES
GALANTES», 1953
Oil, 63¾″ × 44¾″
Private collection

54

THE MUSICIANS, «SOUVENIR DE SIDNEY BECHET,» 1953   Oil, 63¾″ × 44⅞″
Private collection, Paris

PORTRAIT OF ANNE, 1953   Oil, 51″ × 35″   Private collection, Paris

So it is the cold light of the studio in the Rue Gauguet which bathes the new period he enters in 1949 and above all, in 1950. The movement, and one could also say if it did not sound so disparaging, the agitation, of the preceding period has become as it were, fixed. This time the term «composition» covers a subtle and static organization. But that is still infinitely variable, with a reduced palette and with no seeking out of brilliant colors. There is growing observation of the strict rule of «values» as employed by painters who across the centuries, have followed the Venetian School. The heavy impasting allows for every iridescence and gets lighter without however, disguising that tension or violence which we don't find in other painters (no names need be mentioned) who are just as gifted as he is. Are we perhaps, like most of the critics who knew de Staël, influenced by the man's personality? Does his tragic death, coming as it did barely five years later, endow his pictures in retrospect, with their true dimension? It is quite possible. But, in looking at them closely — both at these and the ones produced later — with the perspective of time and with the possibility of comparing them with the production of a whole period, how can we not be aware that they are totally and unexpectedly successful in a way that can never be completely explained?

JACOB'S LADDER

In this third period — the fourth if we consider the *Portrait of Jeannine* and what went before that — we find that all the characteristics and traits we have already put into relief are now fully consolidated: The pure utilization of color, the order of freely blended motifs, the rupture of this same order through an apparent clumsiness of the forms. One could say that de Staël plays on perpetual contradictions: Equilibrium / decentering — thick color / transparency — geometry / free form.

In all the works from this period — which some admirers claim as his best even though he will be much more famous for the work done in the last two years of his life — one has the impression that de Staël, if only because he was a great painter and thus in full control and fully conscious of his methods, was trying to lead us astray, to plunge us into a «noche oscura» where we would find both his torments and those of a pictorial adventure brought to its conclusion.

What is most surprising is that this conclusion is also a flight forward. Having finished with wandering the roads, finished with his battle against poverty, Staël flings himself into conquering the world. He wants exhibitions to be organized, to be written about; he wants to sell and, above all, he wants recognition. Despite all his comings and goings, his constant wheeling and dealing, the breathless correspondence on the shipping of his paintings and other mundane details, he still continues to produce drawings and paintings in enormous quantities, and without ever getting trapped into any formula. If, from one year to the next, it is easy to recognize the signature and unmistakable style (so frequently imitated) of his work, the «compositions» still keep changing, each one being quite different from the last. It is this diversity inside the overall unity of his work which constitutes his genius.

One can see it in the work of 1951. The large, more or less ascensional or pseudo-geometric works are followed by other more fragmented paintings, some of which establish a link with Vuillard and Bonnard. Although the painting in the Museum of Modern Art in Paris entitled *The Roofs* is dated 1952, it was begun long before that and is the final result of a long period of preparation that corresponds to a change in rhythm and speed. It is as if haste and fury had turned to rapid decision — the panting of the runner who has reached his goal. And always the same supreme elegance, the unexpected, and this tension achieved by a wider range of touch, without a wider range of colors, except in their multitude of nuances and selection, more lively — as in the light blues of *The Fugue* in the Phillips Collection in Washington.

For a long time these works were accompanied by some admirable drawings. Close to, and yet independent of the painting, they seem to act like oxygen. On the great white space, lines leap up like a Jacob's ladder; or they suggest the reeds found in Japanese and Chinese art or we get a fine, rich « Pointillisme » where black takes on a thousand hues — or colors in gouache so light that they recall some of Cézanne's drawings. India ink and the discovery of the first felt-tipped pens (of very poor quality, unfortunately) allow for more rapid « writing, » something approaching the results when using the famous Japanese brushes. Staël passes these magic instruments on to Braque, a symbolic exchange that doesn't stop there: Do we not think of Staël when looking at some Varengeville beach painted toward the end of his life by the master of Cubism?

It was through Braque and Zervos, around the beginning of 1951, that Nicolas de Staël made the acquaintance of the poet René Char. They were two of a kind and this was a meeting of two artistic minds each of whom possessed the same sort of intransigent violence. At the time of their meeting Staël had attained the same conciseness as the poet; that « clenched serenity » that is the expression of an entire ethic.

Poets have made common cause with painters since Baudelaire. With Apollinaire, Max Jacob, Paul Eluard, Tristan Tzara, Pierre Reverdy, André Breton, Francis Ponge, the history of French poetry in the twentieth century is inseparable from that of painting. René Char was no exception to the rule: Braque, Picasso, Victor Brauner and, among the younger generation, Vieira da Silva and Wilfredo Lam were all close friends and illustrators of Char. But it seems to me that Char's friendship with Staël was something even deeper, more fraternal. Even if Nicolas de Staël had more intimate friendships as, for example, with Jean Bauret or Pierre Lecuire (whose book we have already mentioned), René Char played an exceptionally important role in the last years of Staël's life which cannot be gauged by the book they produced together nor by the ballet they projected together and for which Stravinsky, Messiaen and Dallapiccola were each successively sounded out.

Nor is it without significance that it was René Char who drew Staël back to the South. The « castle » which Staël would purchase at Ménerbes in 1953 is just a few kilometers from L'Isle-sur-Sorgues, in the heart of that Vaucluse which is Char's homeland. Both of them, albeit through different means and with different personalities, took part in that « search for the base and the summit » — to use the title of a collection by Char wherein he actually pays homage to Nicolas de Staël:

> The field of all and each, too poor, momentarily abandoned,
> Nicolas de Staël puts us in shirt sleeves and in the wind the fractured stone.
> In the chasm of colors he dips it, bathes it, shakes it, creases it,
> The canvas makers of space offer him an orchestra.
> O canvas of rock, who shudders, exposed naked on the rope of love!
> In secret a great painter is going to dress you, for all eyes, with desire the most complete and least exigent.

LANDSCAPE – AGRIGENTO, 1953
Oil, 23½″ × 32″   Private collection, Switzerland

60

THE SUNSET, 1954
Oil, 35″ × 51″   Private collection, Paris

61

One should not look for reciprocal influences between the two men. But the few remaining years left to Nicolas de Staël were to be marked as for René Char, by the same lucid, heart-rending tension.

In 1951, when he was at the height of his creative and artistic consciousness, Staël could reply as follows to a questionnaire sent to him by the New York Museum of Modern Art which had just purchased one of his earlier paintings:

« I want to achieve a harmony. I use painting as my material. My ideal is determined by my individuality and the individual that I am is made up of all the impressions received from the exterior world since and previous to my birth. » And he goes on: « Perception for a painter has

Boats, 1953–54   Drawing, 13″ × 15¾″   Collection of Douglas Cooper

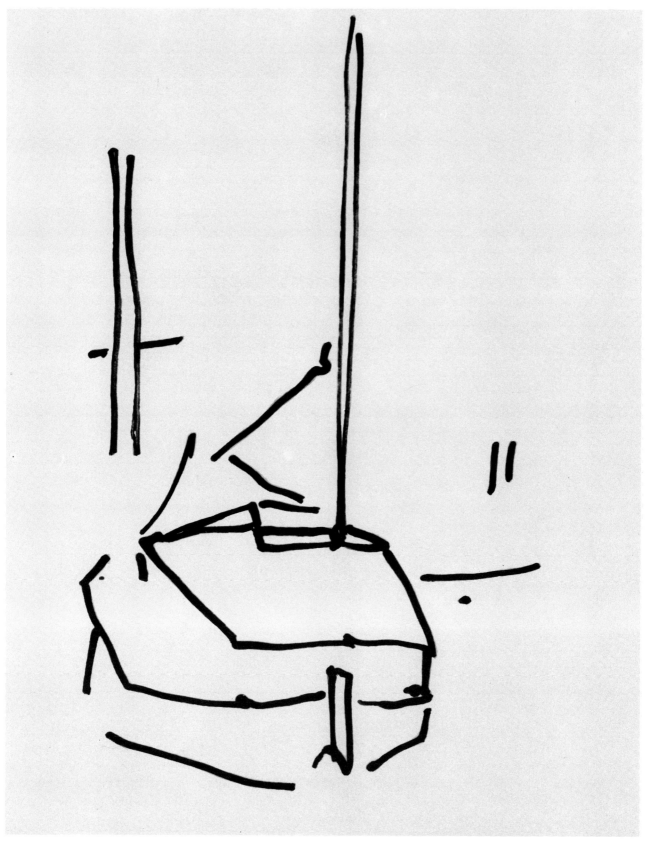

"Flow Master", 1953–54   *Drawing, 12½" × 10"   Private collection*

VASE OF FLOWERS, 1953
Oil, 32″ × 25½″   Private collection

BOTTLES, 1953
Oil, 23½″ × 31¾″   Stephen Hahn Gallery, New York

MARTIGUES, 1954
◁ Oil, 57½″ × 38″   Museum of Winterthur

CAP BLANC NEZ, 1954
Oil, 23½″ × 32″   Stephen Hahn Gallery, New York

THE ARTIST'S TABLE, 1954
Oil, 35" × 45½"   Collection of Mr. and Mrs. Jack I. Poses, New York

THREE PEARS, 1954   Oil, 18″ × 24″
Collection of Mr. and Mrs. Oscar Weiss and Dr. Nigel Weiss, London

only one dimension, that which removes him or draws him to his work. His laborer's hand. I mostly paint without a concept, without conceptual writing. I also start with a clearer image. In both cases, may the perception not be broken in pieces.»

If the 1952 exposition in London marks the beginning of international recognition of Staël's work, the rapid progress of his success in no way affects his need to go on seeking. He has no hesitation, no doubt, as to the subject of his research which imperceptibly, perfidiously, goes beyond a mere pictorial project. The exhausting effort to attain recognition by everyone goes hand in hand with an interior uneasiness that shows no sign of dying away.

The 1950 turning point is neither the first nor the last in a dizzy ascent where for each step the effort would result in a cry of beauty. A certain harmony was followed by new upheavals that other equally great painters of the same period — one thinks in particular of Rothko and Pollock — only expressed in exterior ways. In the successive layers of painting which culminate in the *Roofs* in the Museum of Modern Art in Paris, a blue and red *Landscape* from 1952, the appearance of the first *Bottles,* he seems to return to the exterior world what he had taken from it. The fact is, Nicolas de Staël had already proclaimed: «Always there is a subject, always.» And hadn't the aged Van Dongen already written in 1950, to Georges Duthuit: «When I think of de Staël's paintings, I see a horizontal line, a vast horizon. Above the horizon an immense sky and underneath a meadow, a plain mottled green where tulips sway and there are cows both black and white. . . . The green-gray sea lies in the eyes of our friend. I am unacquainted with his anger, but I can hear the chuckling, side-splitting, sobbing laugh of the wandering urchin and giant that he is.»

Is it henceforth to be simply a question of inverting the process that leads from nature to the concept? We do not believe this was the case. It could be that just when one thinks that Nicolas de Staël is turning his back on Abstractionism he plunges in deeper; that his painting becomes more mysterious.

Bursts of Reality

In 1952, the word «landscape» was already being substituted for the word «composition» in his titles. Perhaps Staël was linking himself with the painters of the past: Hercule Seghers, Delacroix, Van Gogh, Cézanne — the mosaics of Ravenna. Could it be that he was too proud to risk being confused with the painters of his own generation who like himself, had taken by assault the galleries of two continents? But it is true that Staël was looking more and more at the exterior world: The outskirts of Paris — flower markets — the streets of London. Had the moment come for there to be a return to the past? Utrillo? Van Gogh? Or for a frank and proud affirmation that with Nicolas de Staël, the course of painting could begin again?

There can be no definitive answer. Take for example, the best known work from this period: *The Great Football Players of the Parc des Princes* a large composition, 6½ feet by 11½ feet. It was probably the first time that Nicolas de Staël attended a soccer match —a floodlit match, to boot. He who for so long had painted by electric light discovered in reality the violent arti-

Palette Table, 1954   Charcoal, 57″ × 41″   Private collection

FLOWERS IN RED VASE, 1954   Oil, 39½″ × 29″   Stephen Hahn Gallery, New York

ficiality of this green pitch, and the blue and red jerseys. A painter to the depths of his soul and above all, to the depths of his eyes, he projects on the colors and movement of the scene the same look he projects on his canvas. When he gives this minor event an importance it didn't really merit, it is not simply that he wants to demonstrate that reality itself can be abstract. *The Great Football Players,* with two dominant tones, a black and a red, only extends those researches into color rhythm and composition he had already begun and which would be confirmed in the twenty works of this series; each one more « abstract » than the previous one. The shock effect between the choice of the subject itself (which probably owes a lot to Staël's admiration for Roger de la Fresnaye, another painter who died at forty) and his treatment of the subject can only convince the viewer of the absolute autonomy of painting — that quality which Pascal said was its « vanity.»

For Staël it is not painting which is vain, but the exterior world.

The subsequent *«Flowers»* series, then the *«Bottles,»* and his obsession with big Ruysdael skies, are something more than an act of faith toward the tangible world, more than an act of humility toward the sources of inspiration which up until then he would only allow as being in himself. They also demonstrate a supreme disdain for the object chosen: Soccer player, bottle, sky, flowers and, a little later, highways and nudes, it is all the same. Or nearly so. They are what the apples were for Cézanne — and Staël painted those as well. When, with the « Football Player » series, Staël broke through to new principles he was condemned by the defenders of abstract art and enthusiastically praised by the public. But both attitudes, the approving and the disapproving, were based on a misunderstanding. By 1952, it can be said that Staël had really been painting for only ten years, and he had really achieved his own absolute originality during the last three of these. This was painting that never ceased to evolve. The return to the subject was still a way to carry on the struggle with the angel. To paint squares and colored « taches » better than anyone else was to paint in one's own epoch. To paint landscape and still life was to link up with the great paintings of the nineteenth century and, even beyond that, with the Dutch School. It was to do battle on the field of history both for it and against it.

To amplify a rather simple word, painting is much more than painting. One cannot really know Nicolas de Staël without taking into account the profound nostalgia in his soul. The tremendous vitality which his paintings bear witness to, never manages to hide, not even for an instant, and this is what renders them great: The haunting memory of the absolute, the obsession with a question to which, he believed, painting would provide the answer. The breathless succession of these works which no exhibition — no matter how retrospective it may be — can render, was not separable from this idea of a struggle, of « agon,» a hand-to-hand combat between the painter and himself — with, in the middle — the reality which separates his two faces, as in a constantly shattered looking-glass.

Between 1952 and 1955 (the year of his death) Staël knew no rest of either spirit or body. There were journeys to London, to New York (from whence he returned disillusioned), to the north of Italy — with the all-important discovery of Ravenna — to Sicily and Spain. There was the setting up house at Ménerbes and then in Antibes — and there were the constant comings and goings to and from Paris. If one adds to all this the business of organizing exhibitions, the continual search for buyers, the family problems, the needs of friendship, one is simply astonished that he could have continued to produce so much — and all so different[1] — and without ever ceasing to be Nicolas de Staël, recognizable in every chaos, in every outburst.

There had been the grand manner in the paintings of 1950 and 1951. Then came the skies of 1952, the soccer players, bottles and flowers, the strange and distorted views of Le Lavandou, the

---

[1] And no mention is made here of the various attempts at sculpture, tapestry and lithography.

Untitled, 1954–55, Drawing, 14½″ × 12″   Private collection

Untitled, 1954–55, Drawing, 20½″ × 15¾″   Private collection

incredible *Ballet* (7¼ feet by 12 feet). Such productivity, though it may complement what went before, was only the preparation for the following year. More and more «*Skies*», a «*Sea and Cloud,*» a «*Moon*» and that extravagant vision of the «*Indes Galantes*» (which bears very little relation to the show of the same name), beautiful snowscapes, the «*Musicians*» series — of which the «*Souvenir of Sidney Bechet*» is a classic — and finally the nudes, all these seem to mark the galloping days and nights of 1953.

He did not paint more than in previous years and he did not paint any more quickly. The only difference in his way of working was that, compared to the period before the «Football Players» series, he was now in the habit of doing lots of sketches (some were actually nothing more than

Untitled, 1954–55, Drawing, 11½″ × 14″   Private collection

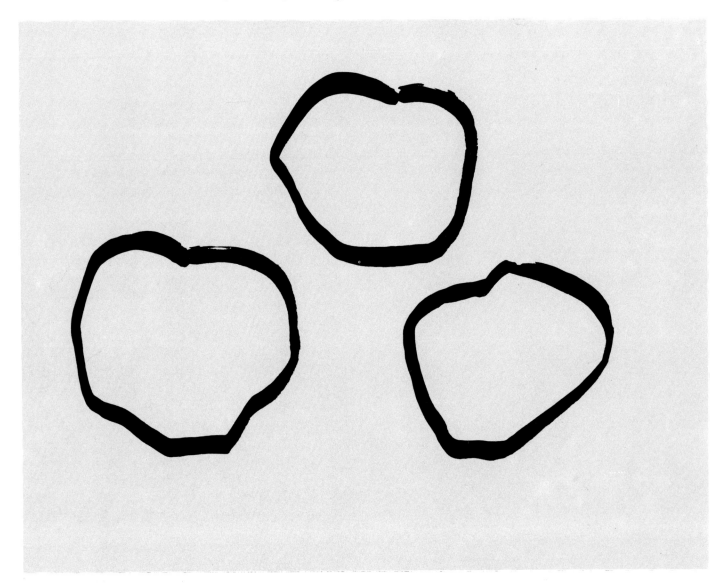

76

RED BOATS, 1954   Oil, 32″ × 22¾″
Milwaukee Art Center, Milwaukee, Wisc. Donated by Mr. and Mrs. Harry L. Bradley

notes in colors) and preparing a series of variations on these, which demonstrate that it was always he, the painter, who was in control of the game when he played with this or that scene taken from reality.

The colors had become explosive, strident, even when he played on the blues and blacks. The impetus toward violence and provocation appeared constantly. The first human bodies to appear in his work — dancers, musicians, «figures» by the seaside — are treated as compact masses, without psychology or anatomy. Look for example, at the silhouettes of Claude Luter and Sidney Bechet. One cannot help but recognize them. But where did Staël get this background of red, yellow, red, blue, and these shapes and musical instruments which are all so similar in fact, to the bottles which he continues to present to us or the bouquets of flowers where he seems to have gathered together the thick color clumps of his older paintings? From Van Gogh perhaps, or Matisse? The series of still-life paintings done at Ménerbes could in fact, draw us back to the history of a recent style of painting to which Staël (a great frequenter of museums) constantly alluded in his letters. But the imprint of his personality is too strong for us ever to find around us anything which resembles a Staël painting — not in the paintings of others (unless of course they are imitators) nor in nature. As was the case during his most «abstract» phase, Staël imposed on his chosen «subjects» his own shapes and his own colors.

The most visible proof of the metamorphosis that he imposed upon reality is the series of views of Agrigento, done when he returned from a trip to Sicily, which stand out as landmarks for the year 1954. Are these abrupt angles and these violet and red roads the country of Empedocles? Most definitely. The homeland of mythology and solar and volcanic fusion but which we can equally well find in the *Roads of Ménerbes* and in the images of *Mediterranean Landscapes*. We should not be afraid to say it: Nicolas de Staël did not become a figurative painter. He was what one calls a «visionary» meaning someone, painter or poet, who sees beyond the appearance of things.

But no sooner has one said that than it must be corrected. «Visionary» can imply pathos, «the idea,» philosophy, suffering or happiness. But there is no literature in Nicolas de Staël and its presence in others annoyed him. To understand this, in reverse, we have to cite extracts from this letter he wrote to Jacques Dubourg on his return from Spain in the fall of 1954:

«. . . I thought a lot about Goya when I was leaving Madrid. If he had had someone to calm him down a bit, he would have been a great painter. For me, you see, the whole business of psychology, social criticism, criticism of character, the annoyance with certain personages, is added on top of the painting, just like an incongruous thing, it is irritating and adds nothing, when it is absent, as in the case of some ordinary admiral or general in polished shoes whom he hasn't the time to criticize, everything is almost marvelous. The same thing for the witches, abortionists, whores and the Duchess. He isn't sufficiently detached from what he does, in spite of his divine hand, because that is beyond discussion, he is divine, it is overpowering.»

And was Staël detached? He would have liked to have been. What he really held against Goya was humanism. It was in fact, the intrusion of that psychological, social and political reality into the realm of painting which he did not see for example, in Courbet: «He is a giant and it will take ages for it to be recognized. I say giant because without esthetics, without conventionalism, without preamble, he produces his unique paintings in a continuous flow, with the same certainty of a river flowing toward the sea, a river which is dense, radiant and sonorous but always sober. Cézanne is a child compared to him.»

Whether one agrees or not with these very arguable judgments — which tell us more about Staël's personality than his taste — what did he have in common with Courbet? One understands

Reclining Nude, 1954–55   Drawing, 42″ × 59″   Private collection

that he wanted to get back to a way of spontaneous painting. If he brings back reality it must be without any contiguous meaning. No more than a bottle signifies drunkenness, a road should not mean escape or walking. «Producing his unique paintings in a continuous flow» may not exactly apply to Courbet but it certainly does to Staël. The return to the subject, the figurative, which did so much for Staël's popularity is only dissembling — a mask — if such expression or word can ever be applied to a man who lived so openly and exposed — to be able to continue expressing himself in a solitude which was growing greater and greater. The more he expresses the exterior world the more he is separated from it. The contact with reality meant that much greater freedom. He becomes henceforth more «fluid» in his painting. And it is only necessary to look at the paintings he left uncompleted to see how his finished works rest on a miraculous balance or on a fullness which the sureness of his eye made final.

RED HORSEMAN, 1954   Oil, 39½″ × 28¾″   Stephen Hahn Gallery, New York

He became aware only gradually of what he was seeking and was eventually to find. The excitement of work, his instability, the brutal changes brought to his life by what he obsessively refers to as «accidents», the sudden departure from Ménerbes for Antibes came as waves of successive shocks to which he reacted like a boxer on the ropes.

Courted by art lovers from all over the world at the precise moment when all art, ancient and modern, had become a speculative commodity, Staël got a contract thanks to Jacques Dubourg, with the famous New York dealer Paul Rosenberg who put on a show in the months of October and November in 1954. His fortune was made. But this also meant that henceforth he was under an obligation to produce, to satisfy the pressing demands of the dealers and art buyers. What painter would be dissatisfied with similar success? Nicolas de Staël for one. In December 1954 he was writing to Jacques Dubourg:

«... What I am trying for is a continuous renewal, but really continuous, and it is not easy. I know what my painting is — underneath its appearance of violence and perpetual forces at play; it is something fragile in the good, in the sublime sense — it is as fragile as love. I also believe, that insofar as I can be in control, I am always trying to take more or less a decisive action regarding my possibilities as a painter. When I throw myself at a big canvas and it turns out well, I have an atrocious feeling, like a vertigo, that too great a portion is by chance, a stroke of luck in the strike of strength, which keeps in spite of everything its aspect of luck, its reverse virtuosity, and that always sends me into miserable states of gloom. I cannot hold on and even the three-meter canvas on which I start out and on which I add a few touches each day after some reflection, all finish in vertigo. I don't master in the true sense of the word, if it has a sense and I would like to be able to strike knowingly, even if I strike as hard and as fast. The important thing is to keep calm as far as one can until the end. If the vertigo which I hold on to as a factor of my quality would turn gently to more conciseness, more freedom, away from harassment, one would have a clearer day. The surprise in a painting or from one period to the next is normal for me — it's as if the things done pass away into a fog once they are no longer there. But who knows maybe that is just a silly dream? It doesn't matter. I will keep the uncertainty of tomorrow until I die, so long as it goes on.»

This shows a stupendous uneasiness, where the words «vertigo» and «luck» are opposed, one can sense, to «conciseness» and «calm» — in short, a desire for mastery and stability in an undertaking that knows no rest, where reflection is constantly being jostled by the shocks of the feelings. This is what one finds in his work in the last phase. The still-lifes, the landscapes, the nudes that suggest both heaviness and transparency (it is as if the gulls cannot fly, nor the ship navigate, nor the nude woman live, nor the brushes in the studio be used for painting) — these are all so many vertigoes; cries congealed in a new sort of beauty to which one can no longer give reference points except that it all represents let us say it once again, both the continuation and the end of great classical painting.

The Struggle with the Angel

Could Nicolas de Staël have won this battle with the angel of which the letter to Jacques Dubourg is but one proof among many? Another person than he, perhaps.... His destiny is

BOATS IN THE HARBOR, 1955
Oil, 28¾″ × 39½″   Private collection, Paris

THE FORT AT ANTIBES, 1955
Oil, 51″ × 35″   Private collection, Paris ▷

the inverse of Van Gogh's, «society's suicide.» There are no pathological signs to be found in Nicolas de Staël. His inability to adapt to social life was greatly compensated for by his appetites and his physical strength which enabled him to dominate people and things.

It is also possible that this strength pushed him to go too far beyond his limits. The old story of the oak and the reed. Secretly and deeply buried, the sickness of death lived inside this restless giant, who in 1951 was already writing to his sister in the convent: «God but life is difficult! One must play on all the notes and play well. Don't believe in the soul, in inspiration, forget secondary schooling, destroy the encyclopedias and do what is simple and good. Jerome's [his son] horse has eyes like the Queen of Egypt this evening. Fool....»

This outline for a scheme of moral and intellectual conduct — the obsession to empty himself of knowledge — preoccupied him more and more, and always in relation to the paintings he was working on. At the beginning of 1955 he wrote to Douglas Cooper:

«One goes on as best one can. And for me to renew myself to develop to go on differently from one thing to the next without *a priori* esthetic ... The important thing is that it should be right. That always. But the more the achievement of this rightness is different from one picture to the next, the more the way that leads to it is absurd, the more I want to follow it ... Too close or too far from the subject — I don't want to be either systematically — and I hold on to that obsession with the dream or the direct obsession itself. I don't know which is better, and I don't give a damm basically so long as it balances off as it can, preferably without balance. I lose contact with the canvas every instant, lose it find it lose it ...

«I just have to believe in accident, I can't make any progress except from one accident to the next. As soon as I feel a logic in it I am annoyed and I veer naturally to the illogical ...

«I believe in luck exactly as I see luck, with a continuous obstinacy. It is also that which makes me see differently from how others see....»

Thus we pass from the pictorial technique to what underlies it and is implied by it. «Accident» and «luck» are not only words which apply to the way such and such a painting «emerges» from him. To understand Nicolas de Staël, to understand his incomprehensible suicide we have to transpose everything he said about painting, or about himself in relation to painting, into the realm of his life. «Obsession,» «balance ... preferably without balance,» «vertigo» have become with Staël the components of a personality which wants to affirm itself as during the time of Romanticism, in its solitude and its uniqueness. We have already said that the «return to the subject,» no matter how ambiguous it may appear, could be explained in part by the desire to differentiate himself from other painters of his time. His flight from Paris, his reactions to the too many commissions that were flowing in, do not signify a wish for failure. As we have seen, Staël gave too much emphasis to the destructive element inherent in his way of painting for him not to be aware of conduct that would have endangered his integrity. Even if we admit — something which is most unlikely — that he felt he could progress no further, having gone too fast, there was nothing to stop him from marking time for a while, something which is quite normal in the life of any creative person.

The recognizably intrinsic qualities of Staël's work are not in truth, separable from the tragedy of which he never ceased to be a part. If he is complete in his paintings it is precisely because his work when it is detached from him, has meaning only in relation to himself.

In the solitude of Antibes interrupted only by storms, Staël, famous and heaped with worldly success, drew deeper and deeper into himself. A certain moment finally came when he no longer understood himself, when he no longer accepted himself.

84

The Gulls, 1955   Oil, 76¾″ × 51¼″   Private collection, Paris   85

THE CONCERT, 1955   Oil, 11½ ft. × 20 ft.   Private collection, Paris

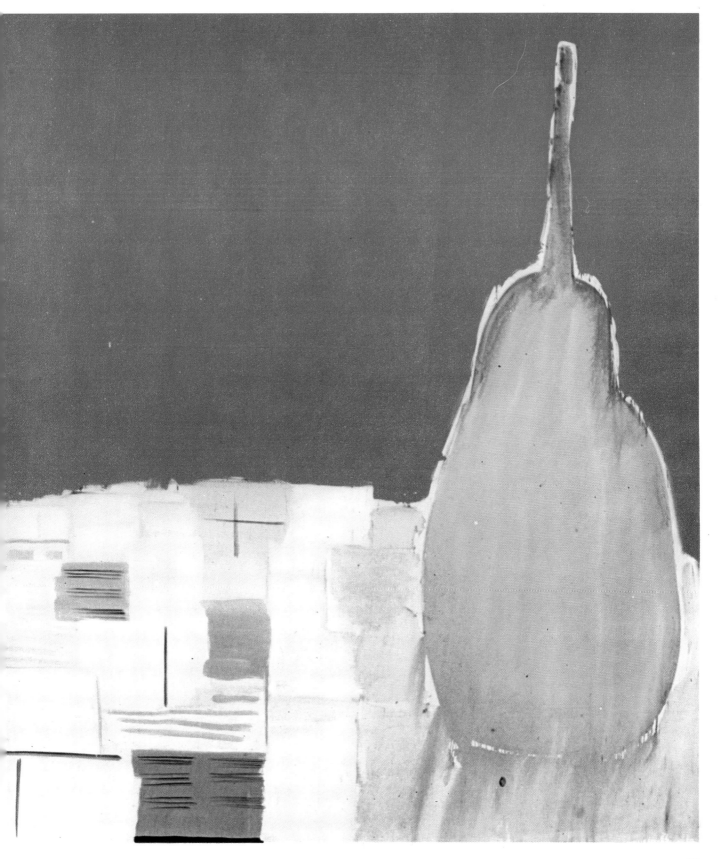

STILL LIFE WITH RED POT, 1955
Oil, 28¾″ × 39½″   Collection of the late Hans Popper, San Francisco, Calif.

88

His health? Three years previously, when he was alone in Paris during the month of August, he thought he had become paralyzed. Nothing serious for someone who used to boast that he could go for eight days without sleep. Stimulants? Alcohol? He swore to his friends that for several months he had touched nothing but fruit juice and he was doing a lot of swimming. Trouble in his private life? There had been. But have we not seen that on the death of Jeannine Guillou, nine years previously, how he had plunged back into life by immediately finding a new companion? And he had just had a son, Gustave, who was born in April 1954.

Nevertheless, he cut himself off from his family and from Ménerbes, that large house where he could have found « peace » — although this was something unknown to him who spoke only of « calm » which is a transitory state.

Probably to escape from himself, he went up to Paris on March 5 to attend a concert of the « Domaine Musical » at the Petit Marigny. He then went back to Antibes and threw himself into two new works inspired by the concert he had « seen » at Paris. One of these, 5¼ feet by 7½ feet, is a black piano with a cello lying beneath it. The painting is unfinished. The other one is enormous: 11½ feet by 20 feet. It was begun in an unused army building in Cap d'Antibes and it too shows the same piano to the left, on a red background, with a double bass and in between a forest of music stands and scores. This painting, which Nicolas de Staël was working on the day before his death, is quite unfinished. In 1972 it was shown at the entrance to the Museum of Modern Art in Paris and its spectral aspect is very much the symbol of death.

He was alone and tired. There had also been talk of sleeping pills. On March 16, 1955, Nicolas de Staël was alone and a prisoner of himself. What went on? He wrote three letters. One to his daughter Anne. One to Jacques Dubourg and the third to his oldest friend, Jean Bauret. The contents of only these last two are known. Here is what he wrote to Jacques Dubourg:

« Jacques,
« I have ordered two chaise longues in wood from a small carpenter near the walls and paid for one, for Ménerbes. The customs still have the little chairs and stool I bought in Spain, also for Ménerbes. The papers are with the company which handled the shipping of my paintings the last time.
« I haven't the strength to carry through my paintings.
« Thanks for everything you've done for me.
« With all my heart.

« Nicolas. »

It is a strange letter, but scarcely a will and testament, in spite of the concern for some everyday details, where the memory of Ménerbes is recalled. There is a sense of lassitude in the second from last sentence. The general expression of gratitude at the end is terrible. This is a simple farewell, a supreme expression of politeness which shows a sense of detachment that none of the other letters of Staël would lead us to expect.

The letter to Jean Bauret is even shorter and leaves no place for explanations or sentiments. It simply shows that, on looking at his life, Staël felt that painting and only painting would be his survival:

« Dear Jean,
« If you have the time would you if any exposition is being organized of my paintings say what has to be done for them to be seen. Thanks for everything.

« Nicolas. »

They are extraordinary leave-takings. More than reticent. But the final gesture is a return — irrational? — to the immoderate violence of this exceptional man. By throwing himself out of his studio window onto the street below, he wants to destroy this body which had served him and was an obstacle in the way of that absolute which he could identify only through his painting. This death is the real signature he puts at the bottom of his works; it authenticates it as much as did that of Van Gogh. He was just forty-one years old. His career as a painter had lasted a bare ten years.

The Hard Rest

Of course, the history of painting didn't stop with Nicolas de Staël. But twenty years after his death we are obliged to note that those contemporaries of Staël who outlived him never found their second or third wind.

Among young painters, irony has taken the place of lyricism. Interest had moved on from Paris to the United States, to London, to Germany. The Paris School has merely survived. Paintings are no longer exhibited at the *Biennales* for young artists.

In truth, the way things are now it would seem that every individual venture or experience is to be condemned. The various « schools » that have followed one after the other in rapid succession since the death of Staël have this in common: They presuppose an immediate complicity not only with other artists but with the public itself. The artist is condemned to be an exhibitionist in a sort of resurrection of Dadaism, a negator of art. This is not to say that some great and violent beauty cannot emerge from such negation — even if only in the theatrical sense — but the act of painting — or sculpting — has scarcely a meaning anymore. The return to anecdote, the use of parody, political manifestoes, the use of scrap and raw materials, no longer allow the artist to express his own particular self through the same means that he had been employing throughout the ages.

When he committed suicide at Antibes in 1955, did Nicolas de Staël foresee this end of a chain of development in which he was one of the last links? No. But nevertheless as things worked out . . .

The external aspects of his death are of little consequence compared to the experience he had lived through in painting like one possessed. Wols died in poverty and alcoholism. America was perhaps too much for Pollock. There is something of historic fate in Staël's death. His own personal contradictions in the end, become a part of the general confusion that followed his death and he could not but have had a premonition of the gathering signs.

His work is firmly placed at the point where the past and the present meet. His « message, » to use a fashionable term, was the same as that of all previous painters — from Rembrandt to Van Gogh, by way of Delacroix. French by adoption, he always affected a deep attachment to French painting — Chardin, Delacroix, Courbet, La Fresnaye, Braque — which denied his own temperament. An abstract painter at a time when the French were belatedly discovering one of the sources of modern art which they had previously neglected, he never ceased returning to the figurative with a vision that was only slightly different from those of his predecessors — at least the Impressionists. The use of color, the subjectivity of the composition — more than the drawing — in many ways belong to the traditions of Abstractionism, but they did not differ funda-

90

Study of Nude in Profile, 1954–55   Charcoal on canvas, 63″ × 44″   Private collection

mentally, from the pictorial tradition. No matter how much he transposed his figures, objects, skies or landscapes they still remained a point of encounter between objective reality and a particular sensibility — which has always been the definition of painting.

One has only to be alone with any of Staël's paintings to understand that this was a battlefield where the conflict went far beyond the wishes and passions of Staël himself. It is the very essence of painting which is in doubt. That absurdity denounced by Pascal, whose name has already been mentioned, can be seen in all its blinding clarity. How can one continue to paint when both reality and painting, in the same creative moment, are questioned? Those painters who preceded Staël, and whom he admired, Braque, Matisse, gave us especially at the end of their lives, a calm view of things. Would Staël have found the same peace if he had lived? We cannot be sure that he would. Unlike the artists we have just mentioned — and the list could be extended considerably — Staël had taken up the battle where Van Gogh had left off. But he differs from the artist who committed suicide at Auvers in that he had put no extrapictorial meaning into his work. Working as he did in the years between 1940 and 1950, in a period when he was forcibly cut off from a civilization which was staggering about in a vacuum finally to come to rest under various forms of collectivism, Staël must have had some obscure intuition that the battle of the solitary artist was then even more desperate than it had been at the end of the nineteenth century.

His strength and his love of life most probably hid this fact. And his achievements are tangible and there to see: The beauty of his paintings and his triumphal success. Staël died like the Marathon runner. He was the winner and he lost. He believed that painting could give him success and self-recognition. Perhaps it was painting that failed. It is not for us to say: We who can still enjoy the pictures — including the unfinished paintings which still haunt the beautiful walls of Ménerbes or the studio in the Rue Gauguet. How can we reproach him for a moment of weakness, for having chosen to be himself; to have allowed himself to have been overcome by a stupidly human failing — despair — though others, but not Nicolas de Staël, would have resigned themselves to plodding on even if the motor was just turning over in neutral?

And what if it was the painter who cracked up rather than the man? Not the one who, in the letter to Jacques Dubourg hadn't «the strength to carry through [his] paintings» but the one who had understood, in a moment of fatigue, solitude and pride, that *even* painting was only vanity. And that if his battle was senseless, then nothing had sense.

There was nothing theatrical about Staël's suicide. This is seen from the last letters he wrote. Consequently there is nothing of the stoic nor of metaphysics in this final gesture which demonstrates, albeit negatively, the existence of something beyond mere appearances. Nevertheless, there is something of all this in his life and death: Romanticism. An attitude which would have been unthinkable at the time when he lived and is even more so in our own day.

And it is in this sense that we say he was the last painter. To expect everything from the art one practices from instinct, and in an exalted state; to rediscover the way to a lost reality through entirely new means, but which are still strictly related to means of expression that will soon be out of date, was an attitude so unusual that it was bound to create severe problems. If we cannot prevent ourselves from looking at Staël's work in the somber light of his death, this does not mean that we can consider his life and work in any way a failure. Quite the contrary.

Of course, at all times in all ages there have been artistic achievements without tragedy. It is not because Staël's life and work are tragic that they are exemplary. It is simply that they can be seen and judged only within a complicated perspective whose outlines are found to be mixed up with a historic fatality and an evolution, the development of which Staël himself wished to retard — or accelerate.

Ten years after his sudden and brutal eclipse and disappearance, René Char wrote:

«Staël's springtime is not something that one can absorb and leave, after a few words of praise, simply because one knows how quickly it passes, how rapidly the downpour stops. The years between 1950 and 1954, because of his work, will appear as years of revival and achievement by one man, whose lot it was to carry out without repose, and in four movements, a search long overdue. Staël has painted pictures. By his own volition he won the hard rest, he endowed us with the unhoped for, which owes nothing to hope.»

SICILIAN HARBOR, 1954   Oil, 44¾″ × 57½″   National Gallery of Canada, Ottawa

BIOGRAPHICAL DATA

1914 Birth of Nicolas de Staël, January 5 (December 23, 1913, in the Gregorian calendar) at St. Petersburg. His father General de Staël, is governor of the Fortress of SS. Peter and Paul.

1916 Nicolas becomes a page at the Court of Nicolas II.

1917 His father is obliged to resign by the Provisional Government.

1919 Exile in Poland.

1921 Death of his father.

1922 Death of his mother near Danzig.

1922–1931 The Staël children are taken in by a Russian family called Fricero in Belgium. Nicolas goes to school in Brussels.

1932–1934 Attends the Saint Gilles Academy and the Royal Academy in Brussels. Early works.

1935 Long journey through Spain. First exhibition at Brussels. Icons and Spanish landscapes.

1937 Settles in Morocco. Reads Delacroix and meets Jeannine Guillou, also a painter, who becomes his companion.

1938 Meets the painter Jean Deyrolle, cousin of Jeannine Guillou, in Brittany. Discovers abstract art.

1939 Works on frescoes as assistant to the painter Fontanarosa. In November he joins the Foreign Legion and is sent to Sidi-bel-Abbès, Algeria, and to Tunisia.

1940 Demobilized from the army, he joins Jeannine at Nice. Meets other abstract painters and takes a variety of jobs to live.

1942 His daughter Anne is born. Paints the *Portrait of Jeannine*.

1943 Moves to Paris and lives in extreme poverty.

1944 Makes friends with Georges Braque, who illustrates a book of poems by Jeannine Guillou's son, Antoine Tudal. Shows his paintings at Jeanne Bucher's, along with Kandinsky and Magnelli. Has his first private exhibition at L'Esquisse Gallery.

1945 Exhibition at Jeanne Bucher's. Participates in the first May Salon.

1946 Death of Jeannine Guillou. Nicolas de Staël marries Françoise Chapouton by whom he will have three children. Moves to Rue Gauguet. Meets the American art dealer Theodore Schempp.

1948 Becomes a naturalized French citizen. Collective exhibition in the Dominican Convent of Saulchoir. Exhibition at Montevideo, Uruguay with an introduction by Pierre Courthion.

1950 Meets Jacques Dubourg who organizes an exhibition of his works. Visits London, where he becomes friendly with Denys Sutton. In Paris he meets Georges Duthuit.

1951 Theodore Schempp organizes an exposition in New York. Roger Van Gindertaël publishes a book on Staël, and Staël's friend, the poet René Char, issues a book of poems illustrated with woodcuts by the painter.

1952 Sees a soccer match at the Parc des Princes and this event will mark Staël's « return to the subject. » Exhibition in London at the Mathiesen Gallery. Works on a tapestry at Aubusson. Spends the summer at Bormes and Le Lavandou.

1953 Travels in Italy (particularly a visit to Ravenna). Goes to New York for an exhibition at the Knoedler Gallery. In August he goes to Sicily and visits Agrigento. Buys a house (Le Castellet) at Ménerbes in the Vaucluse region.

1954 Exposition at the Rosenberg Gallery in New York where he is placed under contract. Moves to Antibes in September. The following month he travels in Spain with Pierre Lecuire. His fourth child, Gustave, is born.

1955 Preparations are made for an exhibition at Jacques Dubourg's. Short visit to Paris. On March 16, Nicolas de Staël commits suicide by throwing himself out of the window of his studio in Antibes.

RETROSPECTIVE EXHIBITIONS*

1955 « Hommage à Nicolas de Staël » at the XI May Salon in Paris.
At the Musée Grimaldi in Antibes.
At the Paul Rosenberg Gallery in New York.

1955–1956 « U. S. Nicolas de Staël. » An exhibition of his work, organized by the American Federation of Arts, travels throughout the United States.

1956 Edinburgh: Exhibition presented by Denys Sutton.
Fort Worth, Texas: Art Center.
London: Arthur Tooth and Sons.
Paris: Musée national d'Art moderne.
Washington, D.C.: The Phillips Gallery.

1957 Berne: Kunsthaus. Presentation by Franz Meyer.
Paris: Galerie Jacques Dubourg.

1958 Arles: Musée Réattu. Presentation by Douglas Cooper.
Paris: Galerie Jeanne Bucher. 42 drawings.

1959–1960 Hannover: Kestner-Gesellschaft.
Turin: Galleria Civica d'Arte Moderna.
(Several exhibitions are held in New York, Zurich and London between 1960 and 1963).

1964 Basle: Galerie Beyeler. Note by Georges Braque.
Paris: Galerie Louis Carré.

1965 Rotterdam: Boymans Museum.
Zurich: Kunsthaus.

1965–1966 Chicago: The Art Institute.

1966 New York: Guggenheim Museum.

1967 Geneva: Galerie Motte.

1972 Saint Paul-de-Vence: Fondation Maeght.

* It would take too long to list the expositions in which Staël participated during his lifetime. The volume published by « Les Editions du Temps » should be consulted for the complete list.

BIBLIOGRAPHY*

BOOKS

COOPER, DOUGLAS: «Nicolas de Staël» (Weidenfeld and Nicolson, London, 1961).

COURTHION, PIERRE: « Nicolas de Staël » (Cailler, Geneva, 1952).

DUTHUIT, GEORGES: « Nicolas de Staël » (Transition Press, Paris, 1950).

GINDERTAËL, ROGER VAN: « Nicolas de Staël » (Hazan, Paris, 1960).

LECUIRE, PIERRE: « Voir Nicolas de Staël » (Pierre Lecuire, ed., Paris, 1953).

SUTTON, DENYS: « Nicolas de Staël » (George Fall, Paris, Grove Press, New York, 1959).

TUDAL, ANTOINE: « Nicolas de Staël » (Le Musée de Poche, 1958).

« Les Editions du Temps » published in 1968 a work, with an introduction by André Chastel, which includes many of Staël's letters, annotated by Germain Viatte, and a descriptive catalog by Jacques Dubourg and Françoise de Staël. This work also provides a list of all the books and articles dedicated to Nicolas de Staël during his life and following his death up until the date of its publication.

PRINCIPAL ARTICLES

CHASTEL, ANDRÉ: « La peinture de Nicolas de Staël » (Le Monde, June 16, 1954).

CHASTEL, ANDRÉ: « Nicolas de Staël à Ménerbes » (Art de France, 1961).

DUMUR, GUY: « Nicolas de Staël » (Cahiers d'Art, 1952).

GRANVILLE, PIERRE: «Nicolas de Staël » (Connaissance des Arts, 1965).

GRENIER, JEAN: « Portrait posthume de Nicolas de Staël » (L'Œil, 1955).

GROJONOWSKI, DANIEL: « Description d'un itinéraire » (Critique, 1966).

RAILLARD, GEORGES: « Staël au Musée Réattu, à Arles » (L'Arc, 1958).

ZERVOS, CHRISTIAN: « Nicolas de Staël » (Cahiers d'Art, 1955).

* See also the catalogs published on the occasions of the various retrospectives of Staël's work, given in the section: Exhibitions.

ILLUSTRATIONS

Artist's Table (The)	68	Marathon	15
« Astronomy »	5	Martigues	66
		Musicians (The)	56
Birds in Flight	46		
Boats	62	Nice	41
Boats in the Harbor	82	« Nocturne »	24
Bottles	55		
Bottles in the Studio	43	Palette Table	71
		« Parc des Princes »	34
Cap Blanc Nez	67	Park of Sceaux (The)	49
Composition	6	Pointillist Landscape	47
Composition	11	Portrait of Anne	57
Composition	13	Portrait of Jeannine	8
Composition	14	Portrait of Jeannine	9
Composition	18		
Composition	22	Reclining Nude	79
Composition	26	Red Boats	77
Composition	27	Red Horseman	80
Composition	31	Red Sky (The)	51
Composition in Black	12	Rue Gauguet	20
Composition in Grey and Blue	21		
Composition on Red Ground	28	Seascape	44
Concert (The)	86–87	Sicilian Harbor	93
		Standing Nude	54
Figures at the Seaside	36	Still Life with Red Pot	88
Flow Master	63	Study at La Ciotat	42
Flowers in Red Vase	72	Study of Nude in Profile	91
Flowers on Black Ground	52	Sunset (The)	61
Football Players	35		
Fort at Antibes (The)	83	Three Pears	69
		Trapped Rocks	17
Gulls (The)	85		
		Untitled	32
« Indes Galantes (Les) »	55	Untitled	38
		Untitled	48
Landscape	30	Untitled	74
Landscape	33	Untitled	75
Landscape	53	Untitled	76
Landscape Agrigento	60		
Landscape La Ciotat	50	Vase of Flowers	64
« Lavandou (Le) »	25		
Light Fragments	10		

ND 553 .S8 D8513 1976

Dumur, Guy, 1921-

Sta¨el

DATE   ISSUED

ND 553 .S8 D8513 1976

Dumur, Guy, 1921-

Sta¨el

DEMCO